world vision
p u b l i s h i n g

PRINTED IN THE UNITED STATES OF AMERICA
All Rights Reserved

Written & Compiled by:
Jeffrey Lawrence Benjamin
Michael B. Kitson
John Oliver
Thomas J. Powell

i

Book design by: Mike Kitson
Cover Design by: Alex Leutzinger, Gilbert Leiker & Annaliese Miller
Cover Photo: John Thomas Ravizé

World Vision Publishing, LLC
COPYRIGHT © 2003, World Vision Publishing, LLC
All rights reserved
Printed in the United States of America
03 02 01 00 99 12 11 10 9 8 7 6

Library of Congress Catalog Card Number: 2003102452
ISBN 0-9727173-1-5

world vision
p u b l i s h i n g

Also by these authors:
Real Life Habits for Success – Achieve Your Goals
Real Life Habits for Success – Break Through Your Stress
Real Life Habits for Success – Master Your Communication

Special Thanks:

Cindie Geddes

Dedication:

This book is dedicated to those people
who want to improve the quality of their lives.

FOREWORD

All it takes is one great idea, one little sentence, a simple concept, reinforced by action, to bring an abundance of prosperity and success into your life. This is the central idea of this book.

We are all created equal in that all of us are blessed with 24 hours a day, 60 minutes an hour and 60 seconds a minute. We all have the same time in a given day. From Bill Gates to Gandhi, from Benjamin Franklin to Mother Teresa to Albert Einstein, right down to you—24 hours in a day!

Throughout history, shadow clocks, sundials, sandglasses and quartz watches have been used to measure time. But what's more important than measuring time is measuring how well that time is spent.

If you're tired of the costs of a cluttered environment, missed appointments, unfinished tasks and projects, procrastination and wasted days, then this book may be the solution to all of your time and life management challenges.

An organized life can mean more time to spend with family and friends, increased earnings, more vacation time, a healthier lifestyle and a greater sense of self-

mastery. Packed within these pages are simple and practical suggestions to help you improve your life. Invest a little time in reading this book, experiment with some of our suggestions and then watch as a world of opportunity opens up before you. You will find that your work, your relationships and your sanity are all improved just by incorporating a few small changes into your thoughts and actions.

Best of success to you!

"The sea is dangerous and its storms terrible, but these obstacles have never been sufficient reason to remain ashore…"

Ferdinand Magellan

HABIT ~ 1

VALUE YOUR TIME

You can't address what you don't recognize. Until you can see time as a valuable commodity, you will continue to waste it. Once you see the value inherent in time you will no more throw it away than you would a hundred-dollar bill. Invest some time in time and write out why you should value yours. Then develop a plan for how to spend your most valuable commodity today and for the rest of your life.

"One of these days is
none of these days."

English proverb

HABIT ~ 2

COMPLETE THE MOST DREADED TASK FIRST

How do you swallow a frog? Don't stare at it too long! A good way to eliminate procrastination is to complete your most dreaded task first thing in the morning. Just get it over with and the rest of your day can be spent on more pleasant tasks and projects.

"Reality is merely an illusion, albeit a very persistent one."

Albert Einstein

HABIT ~ 3

LET EVERYTHING HAVE ITS PLACE

The best way to quickly find your keys, wallet, purse, glasses, etc. is to designate a specific home for each item and then make it a habit of putting things where they belong. The place you choose should be in your direct path of travel (such as a drawer by the primary door you use when leaving). This way the habit seems natural. In time, breaking the habit and putting the item somewhere else will feel awkward and unnatural.

"Our plans miscarry because they have no aim. When a man does not know what harbor he is making for, no wind is the right wind."

Marcus Seneca

HABIT ~ 4

REVIEW YOUR GOALS DAILY

You know where San Francisco is. You know where New York is. But would you try to get from coast to coast without a map? Take the time to write out your goals. Start with the biggest goal you want to achieve and then work back in incremental steps to where you are now. Once your goals have been committed to paper, review them on a daily basis to keep you on track and focused on the life you deserve.

"If I'd never have picked up
the first person,
I'd never have picked up
42,000 in Calcutta."

Mother Teresa

HABIT ~ 5

THINK SMALL TO GET YOU MOVING

Organizing even small projects or areas can save a tremendous amount of time. Don't wait to do it all at once. Waiting around for a nice five-hour block of uninterrupted time to drop in your lap is like waiting around for the perfect stress-free time to quit smoking. It ain't gonna happen. So start small. At home, pick one corner of the house to start in and tackle a small project per week, working clockwise, until every cabinet, drawer, and closet is organized. Use the same strategy in your office using one hour per week for clean up.

"The difference between failure and success is doing a thing nearly right and doing it exactly right."

Edward C. Simmons

HABIT ~ 6

DO IT RIGHT THE FIRST TIME

Carpenters have the right idea: measure twice, cut once. Many people have been known to waste great amounts of time re-doing a task instead of simply doing it right the first time. Whatever it is that you choose to do, resolve to do it right. If you are going to spend the time to do it, take the time to plan it. Sometimes doing things right means doing the best with what you have to work with at the time, then making improvements along the way.

"The actions of men are the best interpreters of their thoughts."

John Locke

HABIT ~ 7

USE YOUR DESK AS A WORK AREA NOT A STORAGE SHED

A cluttered desk creates a cluttered mind. Keep it clean and neat. Don't waste time rummaging through the fallout of a cluttered life just to find a stapler. What is your impression of a person with a messy desk and work area? Does it create or diminish their personal credibility? Set aside a few minutes each day to organize your desk and work area. You'll find it easier to get things done with fewer peripheral distractions.

"Don't mistake movement
for achievement. It's easy to get
faked out by being busy.
The question is –
Busy doing what?"

Jim Rohn

HABIT ~ 8

HAVE YOUR PHONE BE A SERVICE NOT AN INTRUSION

The telephone can be an incredible time saver or a terrible time waster (sometimes both in the same day). To enable your phone to best serve you, set up a system of rules relating to your priorities. Answer and return calls following the system you set up. This works for the office as well as the home. If dinner is the primary time you and your family use to communicate, do not accept interruptions via the phone. The ringer has an off switch for a reason.

"Don't let what you are being get in the way of what you might become."

Harry Palmer

HABIT ~ 9

BE AWARE OF YOUR MOODS

If you're in a great mood most everything seems easy to accomplish, downright exciting. If your mood is low you may struggle with the easiest tasks. Don't buy into your bad moods. Life is always better than what a bad mood may lead you to believe. Stay in balance by making your most important decisions during peak mood times.

"I have found that a person is not a failure due to lack of opportunity, but because of failing to focus attention and resources on the opportunity at hand."

Thomas J. Powell

HABIT ~ 10

COMPLETE WHAT YOU START

Time is a limited resource. It is best to measure the value of completing a project you have started versus that same energy being used toward a new opportunity. Remember that you do not build a house by moving from one foundation to the next foundation; it requires discipline and vision to stay with it until the final touches are complete. The discipline may seem hard at times but the rewards are worth it. It is much easier and more profitable to sell a completed house than it is to sell one with no walls.

"For the things we have to learn before we can do them, we learn by doing them."

Aristotle

HABIT ~ 11

AVOID JUMPING FROM PILE TO PILE

When faced with multiple piles of tasks, always finish what you start. This creates a sense of completion that will drive you to tackle the next pile. You'll experience that there is light at the end of the tunnel. If you jump from pile to pile you'll feel as though you are accomplishing little, which in turn breeds feelings of inadequacy and failure.

"There is nothing which I wish more that you should know, and which fewer people do know, than the true use and value of time."

Lord Chesterfield

HABIT ~ 12

UTILIZE OTHER PEOPLE'S TIME

How much is an hour worth? If you earn $22 on average for an hour of productive activity an hour is worth $22. You can spend that hour mowing the lawn or you can pay a neighborhood kid to do it for you for $10, putting you ahead by $12. When you are faced with multiple uses of your time, look at which add money or fulfillment to your life and do those. Whenever possible, farm out the rest. Most professionals use this tip to increase personal productivity, but it also works to add balance and enjoyment to your limited lifespan.

"A baseball victory is determined not by hits but by runs. The player who gets to third base and no farther doesn't get credit for three-quarters of a run."

Edwin C. Bliss

HABIT ~ 13

BUILD VITALITY THROUGH DAILY EXERCISE

A dull ax will eventually require twice as much effort to cut half as much wood as its sharpened counterpart. The maintenance takes time and effort but more than makes up for the investment in the amount of split wood it returns. Your body is similar to the ax in that it needs to be properly maintained through daily exercise. Moderate aerobic exercise (such as taking a brisk walk) for even one-half hour will help ensure you have enough vitality to meet the possibilities each day holds.

"Without discipline,
there's no life at all."

Katharine Hepburn

HABIT ~ 14

KEEP A GARBAGE CAN NEAR YOUR WORK AREA AND USE IT OFTEN

Don't let procrastination bury you under a mound of paper. Take action on every piece that enters your space. Deal with it, put it in an "in" basket, file it or throw it away! The majority of clutter is related to a reluctance to throw things away. Get in the habit of tossing non-essentials. Not only will it clean up your environment, it will make way for new and better things to enter your life.

"Obstacles are those frightful things you see when you take your eyes off your goals."

Henry Ford

HABIT ~ 15

DO WHATEVER IT TAKES

In order to be successful and fully enjoy life you must be willing to make sacrifices and take consistent action toward your goals and desires. Just about everything you have achieved thus far in life is the result of resourceful thinking coupled with hard work. To get what you want you have to be willing to keep on until the very end, staying on your course, running as hard as you can, bypassing tangents and avoiding potholes wherever possible.

"How use doth breed
a habit in a man!"

William Shakespeare

HABIT ~ 16

UTILIZE THE PROXIMITY PRINCIPLE

It's surprising how most people get up out of their chair to retrieve items they use often, such as staplers, envelopes, general office supplies, reference materials, and the like. Think of your work area (or any other area you want to make more efficient) as a series of concentric circles. Place items you use everyday in the first circle. Let the next circle be for items you use a few times a week, the next for items you use once a month and so on. The more often you use it, the closer it should be. You'll be surprised how much time this saves.

"Compared to what we ought to be, we are only half awake. We are making use of only a small part of our physical and mental resources."

William James

HABIT ~ 17

LISTEN TO AUDIO BOOKS

A fifteen-minute one-way commute twice a day equals 182 hours per year. Make good use of this time by listening to audio books while you drive. Today, more than ever, you can listen to the words spoken by, or about, many of the world's great leaders and philosophers. Audio books are a great way to increase the retention of material you have read, or can be used to expand your current volume of knowledge. Buy them at local bookstores (or on-line) or check them out from your local library.

"Chaos often breeds life,
when order breeds habit."

Henry Brooks Adams

HABIT ~ 18

USE A FILE CABINET

Place your monthly statements and other paperwork in files for easy storage and reference. To reduce clutter and increase efficiency, get folders with fasteners to prevent paperwork from falling all over the place when you open the file. This is an especially useful tool when working with chronological paperwork. It also prevents important papers from getting lost. Then once your files are orderly, put them in order. Chronologically, alphabetically, prioritized—find a system that makes sense for you and then stick to it.

"Every calling is great
when greatly pursued."

Oliver Wendell Holmes

HABIT ~ 19

HIRE A PERSONAL FITNESS TRAINER

Take advantage of the knowledge and experience of a professional. Whether you are just getting back into shape or you're a top-level athlete, that little extra push may be just what you need to reach the next level. A personal trainer provides you with the skills, the motivation and the enthusiasm to help you stay fit and healthy. Exercising the right way for half an hour is much better than doing it the wrong way for twice that long. Let an expert teach you the right way. And never underestimate the power of an appointment to keep you to your exercise goals. Being responsible to another person is a great motivator!

"Find and nurture the love
in all whom you meet."

John R. Oliver

HABIT ~ 20

OFFER YOUR LOVE TO OTHERS

Take the time to love someone who is hard to love—the surly waiter (maybe making minimum wage and working too hard for the idiot who occupied your seat before you), the cranky co-worker (who may be struggling with a family illness), the rebellious teen (who is likely simply trying to figure out how to be a grownup). This person probably needs love the most. Start with strangers who are less than friendly and progress to individuals you know but just don't care for. You will both grow from the experience. And don't forget those you love the most. Love is easy for them, time may be harder.

"Efficiency is only truly great
when it is focused
on effectiveness."

Thomas J. Powell

HABIT ~ 21

SYSTEMIZE ROUTINE TASKS

One of the biggest time wasters is stepping over the same territory time after time after time. Track your steps throughout a day and see how many tasks cause you to spend time traveling to and from a destination, then look for ways to improve the efficiency of such travels. This can be as simple as how many times you get up to fax items or as big as picking up the kids from school and dropping them off at practice. By simply coming up with a system for routine tasks you will dramatically change your effectiveness.

"Zeal without knowledge
is fire without light."

Thomas Fuller

HABIT ~ 22

SEE EVERYONE AS A TEACHER

It is your responsibility to determine what the lessons are in every experience. When you do this you will find yourself far less annoyed or frustrated by the comments or actions of others. Change your thinking from "Why is someone doing this or that?" to "What can I learn from this?" You may find that this can bring you peace and balance. You may also find you pick up lessons from small cues rather than large ones. Better to learn empathy from the stranger annoying you in line than from the serious illness of a close friend. One way or another you will learn the lessons you need in life.

"Seize the very first opportunity to act on every resolution you make, and on every emotional prompting you may experience in the direction of the habits you aspire to gain."

William James

HABIT ~ 23

CONSOLIDATE ALL CALENDARS AND APPOINTMENT BOOKS

Place all floating pieces of paperwork, all information, in one calendar organizer. Avoid using several calendars for appointments and deadlines. Make your life easier by consolidating this important information into one easy-to-reference organizer. You can buy an organizer at your local office supply company or visit www.franklincovey.com to review what it has to offer. Whether paper or electronic, if you use it right, you need only one organizer.

"We are not interested in
the possibility of defeat."

Queen Victoria

HABIT ~ 24

TAKE A POWER NAP

Being fatigued is one of the biggest time stealers you will encounter. Fatigue can cause you to make mistakes, work slower or not even enjoy the present moment. Simply closing your eyes for 15 to 20 minutes will give you a fabulous recharge. But be careful not to nap for longer than thirty-five minutes as you may wake up feeling groggy.

"It seemed rather incongruous
that in a society of super
sophisticated communication,
we often suffer from
a shortage of listeners."

Erma Bombeck

HABIT ~ 25

OPEN YOUR EARS AND LISTEN

Shut up and save time. People will usually give you the information you're in search of if you allow them to complete their thoughts and explanations. Good communication starts with active listening and in fewer errors and less time redoing botched jobs. Listening is the best way to learn. Those who learn to listen with the intent to completely understand are the most loved and respected.

"It takes less time to do a thing right than it does to explain why you did it wrong."

Henry Wadsworth Longfellow

HABIT ~ 26

USE A ROLODEX OR SETUP AN ELECTRONIC DATABASE

Countless people get frustrated when not being able to locate an important phone number or address. Seconds stack up into minutes which stack up into hours of wasted time and effort. Invest some time in creating an electronic database for phone calls and mailings. Get all your addresses and phone numbers organized into one place, update them regularly and remember to keep it all handy.

"In my relationships with persons I have found that it does not help, in the long run, to act as though I were something that I am not."

Carl Rogers

HABIT ~ 27

HIRE A PROFESSIONAL

Seeking help from a professional can save you lots of time (and money). Employ the services of a good accountant, contractor, lawyer, doctor, plumber and the like. These people perform tasks everyday that you might attempt once a year. Who do you think is going to be more efficient? Too many people attempt to do-it-themselves only to find that their performance is mediocre or downright destructive. Oftentimes a professional is called in only after the situation has turned into a total disaster.

"It is necessary to the happiness of man that he be mentally faithful to himself."

Thomas Paine

HABIT ~ 28

LIVE AN HONEST LIFE

Do you ever find yourself twisting words and thoughts with the intent to deceive? Or worse, did you realize it only after the fact? How much time and energy did this cost you in the end? The adage, "The truth will set you free" is not meant for the benefit of mankind but for the benefit of you. Being truthful to yourself and others saves you time and reputation. Truthfulness will bring you a sense of peace. And it will save you all that time and effort of backtracking, re-spinning or trying to keep your stories straight.

"There is only one corner of
the universe you can be certain
of improving, and that's
your own self."

Aldus Huxley

HABIT ~ 29

EAT HEALTHY WHOLESOME FOODS

Healthy living is a choice that starts by convincing yourself to eat nutritious food versus eating junk food. Start by deciding what benefits you will receive from maintaining a balanced, nutritional, life-long eating habit. Keep fruit, vegetables, snack bars and low-fat yogurt handy for you to reach for throughout the day. If this proves too difficult for you, analyze what's really happening. What hole in your life are you trying to fill with food? Why do you not think you are worth treating with the same respect and care you would treat your dog or your car?

"Men's natures are alike;
it is their habits that
carry them far apart."

Confucius

HABIT ~ 30

PLAN FOR THE NEXT DAY

Gain a clearer understanding of what you are prepared to accomplish on your next day's business schedule. Have you ever seen a chicken with its head cut off? It runs around, darting from place to place, much like a crazy man bouncing off walls in a padded room. Sound familiar? The cliché did not come into vogue for nothing. Take the time to plan your next day of business, the day before. A little preparation goes a long way.

"Success seems to be largely a matter of hanging on after others have let go."

William Feather

HABIT ~ 31

PRACTICE PATIENCE TO SAVE TIME

Patience is the catalyst for balance and time saving accuracy. Exercising patience can improve any situation, from driving to following instructions, waiting in line to figuring something out, listening, dressing your children, preparing a speech or document. The list is infinite. Getting frustrated and angry doesn't make the person in front of you drive faster or the computer stop feeding you error messages. If you can't change the situation, take a deep breath, calm down and enjoy the view.

"Sow a thought, and you reap an act;
Sow an act, and you reap a habit;
Sow a habit, and you reap
a character; Sow a character,
and you reap a destiny."

Samuel Smiles

HABIT ~ 32

ALLOCATE TIME FOR EACH AREA OF YOUR LIFE

Define how much time you are committed to allocating to each area of your life. For example, health 25%, family 25%, work 35%, community involvement 15%. Imagine if each area of life were like a spoke in a wheel. If you remove or lose one or two spokes, your wheel begins to wobble and efficiency diminishes. A well-rounded life, giving attention to all areas, is what makes one feel successful.

"One of the very nicest things about life is the way we must regularly stop whatever it is we are doing and devote our attention to eating."

Luciano Pavarotti

HABIT ~ 33

EAT SMALL MEALS VERSUS FEASTS

Do you like the feeling of being bloated from eating a large meal? It feels gross and it creates plenty of health problems too. The key to eating more is eating less. If you love to eat, like most of us, eat smaller meals throughout the entire day. This habit burns calories more efficiently and keeps your energy level high. Eat slowly and with presence of mind. Enjoy each meal and be conscious of what it is you are putting into your body. Staying present at mealtime can not only change what you eat, but how you feel about food in general.

"Success comes to those who become success conscious. Failure comes to those who indifferently allow themselves to become failure conscious."

Napoleon Hill

HABIT ~ 34

PERFORM, PRACTICE AND PLAY

When looking at your schedule, categorize your days as a performing artist or athlete does: Performance Days, Practice Days and Play Days; then utilize the day appropriately. Performance Days should be reserved for your most productive activities, Play Days for rejuvenating and Practice Days for making the most of your Performance and Play days. Letting your days run together is like letting Neapolitan ice cream get warm eventually it just looks like mud.

"If you say what you think,
don't expect to hear
only what you like."

Malcolm Forbes

HABIT ~ 35

ALLOW OTHERS TO FULLY EXPRESS THEMSELVES

Being right! If you truly want balance in your life let others feel as if they are right most of the time. Allowing others to fully express themselves with no reaction from you not only saves time but nurtures balance. For one week challenge yourself to not argue, explain your side, cut others' speech short, rationalize, disagree, relive situations, talk belligerently, complain or any other self-righteous act in which you may find yourself engaging.

"Practice and thought
might gradually forge
many an art."

Virgil

HABIT ~ 36

REVIEW AND TRANSFER ANY UNCOMPLETED ACTIVITIES

A task only becomes a habit with daily use. Daily use takes a little bit of planning. Make it a point to transfer uncompleted tasks at the end of the day to your next day's to-do list. This allows you to focus on what needs to be done. When things start to seem a little overwhelming, remember that you only have to accomplish one task at a time. But if you find yourself transferring an item more than four times consider whether it is important or whether it needs to be moved to a long-term to-do list.

"I am not afraid…
I was born to do this."

Joan of Arc

HABIT ~ 37

WEIGH THE FACTS AND DECIDE

You've heard the phrase: analysis paralysis. Indecision is caused by the fear of making a wrong choice. Knowledge is power over the unknown. The more you know about a subject, the more confident you feel and the more likely you are to make the right choice. Take control over your fear and over your destiny by acquiring the knowledge you need. Gather all the information and facts you can on the subject at hand, review them, then make your decision. If it helps, choose a specific time frame in which you will render your decision.

"The wise will always
reflect on the quality,
not the quantity of life."

Marcus Seneca

HABIT ~ 38

MEET FOR COFFEE VERSUS LUNCH

A business lunch often takes one and a half to two hours of time. A great option to the standard business lunch is to meet over coffee. Most coffee houses provide comfortable chairs and tables and some even have conference rooms for public use. After you order your coffee you are able to focus on the business at hand and the person with whom you are meeting instead of on the meal you are eating. Plus you never have to worry about having spinach caught in your teeth or whether your table manners are up to the challenge of the three forks flanking your plate.

"No great man ever complains
of want of opportunity."

Ralph Waldo Emerson

HABIT ~ 39

SEPARATE THE MAJORS
FROM THE MINORS

Make a priority list and then compare the time you spend relative to that list. If you are spending a majority of your time on minor things it is time to make a change. Track your time. Track your priorities. Try to get these two tracks to match so your actions more closely match your goals. Since you are the only one living your life you are the only one with the power to choose how you spend your time.

"Only those who are able to
relax can create, and then
ideas reach the mind
like lightening."

Ciero

HABIT ~ 40
KICK BACK AND RELAX

You will accomplish more and gain accuracy in everything you do by maintaining a relaxed demeanor. Your decision-making is enhanced and you don't get flustered as easily. You just plain feel better. The road to efficiency is paved with relaxation techniques. Experiment and find yours. Burn incense, exercise, write poetry, listen to soothing music, try yoga or tai chi, paint or sculpt, sit in a hot tub — whatever healthy activity it takes for you to maintain a relaxed state. For more ideas consult *Real Life Habits for Success: Break Through Your Stress.*

"Confidence in ourselves
is perhaps the single most
important ingredient for
leading a life of success
and happiness."

Jeffrey Lawrence Benjamin

HABIT ~ 41

WALK WITH CERTAINTY

Avoid shuffling or being dragged toward opportunity when it presents itself. Unfortunately, most people sell themselves short. Develop the confidence in yourself to meet opportunity head-on. And when you lack confidence, fake your way back. When you begin to feel a little uncertain, simply assume a mental state of confidence, stand up straight, take a breath and walk toward your opportunity with certainty.

"Happiness is a dividend on a well-invested life."

Duncan Stuart

HABIT ~ 42

BECOME MORE VALUABLE

A person does not truly earn an hourly wage; they earn a wage relative to the amount of labor performed and the value of that labor, exchanged for one hour of that person's life. Some people have the skill set and opportunities to earn a minimum wage while others earn hundreds, thousands, and even millions of dollars for the same hour of investment. You can choose to become more valuable simply by investing your time into learning new skills and embracing new opportunities. Learning is an investment in your future. Are you worth it?

"Practice is the best
of all instructors."

Publilius Syrus

HABIT ~ 43

SEPARATE YOUR PERSONAL AND BUSINESS TIME

When conducting business avoid working on personal stuff, when enjoying personal time avoid work concerns. It's easier said than done, but with practice you can do it. Most people unconsciously melt these areas of life together which ends up causing them stress and grief. The people who take their personal problems to work inhibit their performance, while those constantly working on business lose quality of life. Know when to draw the line and then do it!

"I'm an idealist.
I don't know where I'm going
but I'm on my way."

Carl Sandburg

HABIT ~ 44

LEARN TO DEAL WITH THE TRAFFIC

Choose to make driving a relaxing and rejuvenating peaceful experience. Traffic is what it is. Only you can give it the power to anger you. Start toward your destination with plenty of time to spare. Find the positives in the experience — time to yourself, peace and quiet to hear your own thoughts, opportunity to catch up on the news, music or books on tape. Set yourself up to enjoy each drive or commute. Say to yourself as you buckle your seat belt, "I love my driving time" and soon you will.

"Live your own life, for you will die your own death."

Latin Proverb

HABIT ~ 45

KEEP A WRITTEN RECORD OF YOUR LIFE

Record your daily events, thoughts and ideas in a journal. Find a blank book whose design truly speaks to you—leather bound with gilded pages, flowers with rough pink paper, plain black composition book, or custom designed—the variety is virtually endless. And have a good pen—ball point, fountain, gel, roller ball, calligraphic, wildly colored inks, conservative black and blue—experiment with what makes you feel creative. Save the last three pages of each book to index your writings.

"Men do less than they ought,
unless they do all
that they can."

Thomas Carlyle

HABIT ~ 46

BLOCK OUT TIME TO GET THINGS DONE

One of the best ways to get things done is to block out specific times for certain tasks and projects. For example, from 8am to 11am make and take phone calls; from 11am to 12pm catch up on some paperwork. From 4:30pm to 5:00pm write your to-do-list for the next day. Make sure you block-out personal time! Balance is the bliss of the universe.

"Men are born to succeed—
not to fail!"

Henry David Thoreau

HABIT - 47

LAY OUT YOUR CLOTHES FOR THE NEXT DAY

To start out the morning without feeling rushed, lay out your clothes the night before. Make sure each item is ironed, stockings matched, and your shoes are shined. It is amazing how much smoother your morning will be and how much more put together you will look (no more showing up with one navy sock and one black because you were rushing to find a match).

"I would rather be able to appreciate things I cannot have than to have things I am not able to appreciate."

Elbert Hubbard

HABIT ~ 48

GIVE IT AWAY

Each year clear out your garage and closet, and give it away. If you haven't used it, worn it or treasured it in a year, out it goes! Drop it by the Salvation Army or some other charitable organization (some will come to you for pickup). The act of giving away what you don't absolutely cherish or can't live without is a reward in itself. If you choose to do this you will surely experience numerous intangible and serendipitous exchanges.

"There are no
ordinary moments."

Dan Millman

HABIT ~ 49

ACCOUNT FOR YOUR CURRENT TIME USING A TIME LOG

How, where, and on what do you spend your time? The best way to get a grasp on your time is to log your time showing how it is used. What is it that you do during your day, week or month? Logging your time allows you to clearly understand where you are spending your time, how you can eliminate time wasters and how you can realign your time with your goals.

"Trying is just a noisy way of not doing something."

Anonymous

HABIT ~ 50

READ PERSONAL DEVELOPMENT BOOKS

Reading is one of the best ways to expand your mind. Here are some recommendations: *Think & Grow Rich* by Napoleon Hill, *Awaken the Giant Within* by Anthony Robbins, *The 7 Habits of Highly Effective People* by Stephen Covey, *Real Magic* by Dr. Wayne W. Dyer, *Being The Best* by Denis Waitley, *Chicken Soup for the Soul* by Jack Canfield and Mark Victor Hansen. Get other recommendations from friends and colleagues and start learning which styles work for you.

"He who desires but acts not breeds pestilence."

William Blake

HABIT ~ 51

CREATE AND USE CHECKLISTS

This habit alone will save you numerous hours. Whether you're going camping, hosting a special event, flying a plane, preparing for a race, packing for vacation or getting ready for a sales presentation, a checklist will help you stay organized and on track to achieve what you want. A checklist allows you to make mistakes on paper as you plan rather than on the tasks you hold dear.

"All things are possible until they are proved impossible— and even the impossible may only be so as of now."

Pearl S. Buck

HABIT ~ 52

EMBRACE CHANGE—NOW

Welcome change. If you have ever experienced the frustration of fighting change you may understand the futility of your efforts. In these times of rapid change you can quickly find yourself out of balance and wasting time attempting to prevent change. Change is coming, be ready to accept and embrace it. Obsolescence (in your physical, personal or business life) is a killer. If you have any doubts about that, sit back, do nothing and let the reaper have at you, for there will always be others willing to learn, adapt and grow to take your place.

"Attempt the impossible
in order to improve
your work."

Bette Davis

HABIT ~ 53

ESTIMATE HOW LONG IT WILL TAKE TO COMPLETE A TASK

Before beginning a task, estimate how long it will take to complete it. For tasks you are not completely familiar with, take that estimate and double it. Then schedule time in your calendar organizer for completion. You can complete the task in one session or allocate time in increments, whichever suits your style and energy levels as well as the task itself.

"It is not enough to
have a good mind. The main
thing is to use it well."

Rene Descartes

HABIT ~ 54

GET OFF YOUR BACK

Have you ever lost your cool? Of course, we all loose it and revert to being angry, stressed, frustrated and neurotic. What is important is that we learn something from our flair-ups. Every mistake is a learning opportunity. Give yourself a break, laugh and move forward having learned a valuable lesson instead of wasting time beating yourself up.

"Industry is the soul of business and the keystone of prosperity."

Charles Dickens

HABIT ~ 55

BUY AND USE SUPPLIES THAT GET YOU ORGANIZED

Visit your local office supply store and purchase items you feel may help you get and stay organized. Search through every aisle in the store to find items such as color-coded files, file racks, index card systems and telephone message pads. Buy and use whatever it takes to get you organized. Experiment with different products and different systems to find what works best for you. Are you a very visual person? Try color-coding everything you can. Are you more stimulated by sound? Try a variable set of alarms to remind you of appointments and tasks.

"I personally measure success in terms of the contributions an individual makes to her or his fellow human beings."

Margaret Mead

HABIT ~ 56

WALK A MILE IN YOUR NEIGHBOR'S MOCCASINS

Express sincere compassion on a daily basis. Simply put yourself in someone else's shoes as often as possible. The balance this will help you gain in your own life is immeasurable. Make a list of what you can do to show empathy and compassion. Help a friend with a chore or project, smile at a stranger, volunteer for anything or just be a good listener. The list can (and should) be endless. Express compassion and enjoy the balance this brings you. Best of all, prepare to receive what you give.

"Fortune is ever seen
accompanying industry."

Oliver Goldsmith

HABIT ~ 57

PREPARE AND FOLLOW AN AGENDA

It's amazing how many limitless hours seem to be spent in unproductive meetings. Billions of dollars are flushed down the drain, valuable time is wasted and frustrations grow as busy people watch their lives tick away to the droning of yet another poorly planned, poorly executed and inevitably useless meeting. One of the best ways to make a meeting productive is to plan an agenda and then stick to it. Keep it short and to the point. Brevity is the soul of productive meetings. Take notes on what is discussed and then use those notes as a springboard for future agenda items.

"If you can conceive it
in your mind,
then it can be brought
into the physical world."

Dr. Wayne W. Dyer

HABIT ~ 58

PRACTICE YOUR POWER OF CHOICE

If you are less than thrilled with your present lot in life you are not alone. However, it is your choice to spend your time doing what feeds your soul or what sucks the life out of you. Plan and take consistent daily action toward the life you envision. Write out your vision for the future and resolve to stop complaining about what is and blaming what was. What will be is always your choice.

"Diligence is the mother
of good fortune, and idleness,
its opposite, never led to
good intention's goal."

Miguel de Cervantes

HABIT ~ 59

MIX UP YOUR WORK TO BREAK MONOTONY

Avoid brain drain by mixing up your tasks and projects throughout your day. Change activities about every three hours to maintain interest and to keep an optimum energy level. Changing tasks and then returning back to them provides you with a new, more empowering perspective that will help take you to the next level.

"Drop the question what tomorrow may bring, and count as profit every day that fate allows you."

Horace

HABIT ~ 60

SCHEDULE TIME TO DO NOTHING

Few of us take the time to just do nothing. Scheduling time to do nothing allows your mind to get centered. It will also allow you to remember all the things for which you are grateful. Most people get frazzled from spinning out of control in their personal and business life. Schedule time to "vegetate" and remove yourself from the hustle and bustle of life. Recharge and rejuvenate so that you don't become an empty vessel with nothing left to give.

"Would you live with ease,
do what you ought, and not
what you please."

Benjamin Franklin

HABIT ~ 61

LEARN TO SAY "NO"

Learning to say no can be one of the most difficult habits to acquire. One of the main reasons people never achieve their goals is because they are too busy helping other people achieve theirs. Helping others is what life is about, but not at the expense of sacrificing what is important to you. Again, it's about balance. Say "no" to anything that does not fulfill you, advance you toward your goals or make you happy. Don't bother with excuses or apologies. A simple "no, but thank you for asking," will suffice.

"If you understand,
things are just as they are;
if you do not understand,
things are just as they are."

Zen Proverb

HABIT ~ 62

UTILIZE TECHNOLOGY

Using an electronic scheduling program on your computer that includes a task management and address system will save you a tremendous number of hours each year. When you combine the desktop technology with a handheld component you step up your efficiency again. The technology saves you from having to write recurring tasks, it enables you to search exact times and dates in seconds, keep a conversation and delegation log, and it can automatically create a backup file that can be restored in case your data is lost. Best of all, it allows you to combine most of life's loose papers into one easy to carry package.

"The successful man lengthens his stride when he discovers that the signpost has deceived him; the failure looks for a place to sit down."

J.R. Rogers

HABIT ~ 63

TURN FRUSTRATION INTO FASCINATION

This doesn't usually save time, but it surely makes those frustrating times much more tolerable. When you choose the slow line at the grocery store and you are in a big hurry, simply smile and say, "Isn't this fascinating?" Do the same thing when you are traveling on the freeway and the traffic is at a dead stop, or your plane is delayed, or your doctor is behind schedule. Looking at the situation and the part you are playing in it, as fascinating will change your attitude and at least make the time seem to go faster.

"Over-commitments are for under-achievers."

Jeffrey Lawrence Benjamin

HABIT ~ 64

SET FEWER GOALS

Failure often comes from spreading yourself too thin. Success comes from having a realistic understanding of your limitations. There are only so many hours in a given day, and there are unlimited amounts of opportunity as well. We can't achieve everything yet we can achieve the things that are the most important to us. If you find that you are not able to achieve the things that you want, then it's time to reduce the number of things you want to achieve. Move forward on new goals only after you have achieved the ones you have already set for yourself.

"There is nothing so useless
as doing efficiently that which
should not be done at all."

Peter F. Drucker

HABIT ~ 65

PRACTICE ACTIVE DELEGATION

Delegate! The art of delegating enables you to expand the number of tasks you can complete in a day and allows others the chance to learn and experience ownership in a project. The best leaders and achievers are those people who surround themselves with competent people to whom they can assign projects and tasks. Practice these three key ingredients to effective delegation: make sure your instructions and desired results are clear, give the person to whom you delegate the freedom and authority to complete the task, and make sure you don't get the same project delegated back to you through your own attitude of: "it's easier to do it myself."

"As tools become rusty,
so does the mind;
a garden uncared for
soon becomes
smothered in weeds;
a talent neglected
withers and dies."

Ethel R. Page

HABIT ~ 66

CARRY HANDY READING MATERIAL

Use the time you spend while stuck in line at the bank or in the waiting room at the dentist's office expanding your knowledge through reading. You'll be able to read two extra books a year by keeping material with you that you can read in small bites. Paperbacks are great for this, as are the new lines of electronic books, some of which can even be read on a hand-held electronic organizer.

"Parents can only give good advice or put them on the right paths, but the final forming of a person's character lies in their own hands."

Anne Frank

HABIT ~ 67

PLACE A FAMILY CALENDAR ON YOUR REFRIGERATOR

Reduce the chaos in your home by utilizing a family calendar. From the kids to your spouse to the dog, everyone has places to be, people to see and things to do. A centrally located family calendar can help ensure that obligations such as the kids' ball games, dinner with friends, doctor or vet appointments or a family night are all met.

"Let me tell you the secret that has led me to my goal: my strength lies solely in my tenacity."

Louis Pasteur

HABIT ~ 68

USE A "DO NOT DISTURB" SIGN

Focus the majority of your attention on active paperwork and projects. Get rid of clutter, reduce interruptions and get organized. This all takes time, but gives back more time for the priorities in your life. If it helps, place a do-not-disturb sign on your door (even at home) or on the outside of your cubicle to let people know you are in focus time. Teach the people around you to take the sign seriously by taking it seriously yourself. Do not allow disturbances or distractions (internal or external). Let bosses and emergencies be the only exceptions.

"Diamonds are only lumps
of coal that stuck
to their jobs."

B. C. Forbes

HABIT ~ 69

HIRE SOMEONE TO HELP YOU GET ORGANIZED

The job of organization can be overwhelming at times, so get some help when you need it. For every task there is an expert. From organizational gurus to clutter consultants to a temp to help with filing for a day, there is someone who can get you on track. But only you can keep you on track.

"Most people are about as happy as they make up their minds to be."

Abraham Lincoln

HABIT ~ 70

BE HAPPY NOW

What good reason do you have for postponing your happiness? Maybe you would be happier if you had a nicer car or house, perhaps if you lost weight, had more money or got the job of your dreams. Maybe not. The truth is: this is the best time to be happy, regardless of what you may conjure up to hold you back. It's your choice: neurotic or happy!

"What would be the use of
immortality to a person
who cannot use well
a half hour?"

Ralph Waldo Emerson

HABIT ~ 71

KNOW YOUR INTERNAL CLOCK

Each of us has an internal clock that operates better for specific tasks during certain times of the day. Know your rhythms and then schedule your time appropriately. For example, maybe you concentrate better in the morning and your mind wanders in the afternoon. So do the big projects in the morning and save the smaller ones for later.

"I never see failure as failure
but only as a
learning experience."

Tom Hopkins

HABIT ~ 72

GIVE YOURSELF THE OKAY TO FAIL

Procrastination sets in when you entertain thoughts of perfection or fear of failure. View each experience as an opportunity to learn and grow. Think in terms of progress, knowing that each step and stumble takes you closer to your destination. It may not always be pretty but we learn from failure as well as from success. That's how we grow. In nature, what doesn't grow dies. You are part of nature.

"It is useless to desire more
time if you are already wasting
what little you have."

James Allen

HABIT ~ 73

PERFORM TASKS AND ERRANDS STRATEGICALLY

Plan and perform your tasks and errands strategically. Reduce the number of times you have to backtrack or repeat trips. In order to make the most of your time, think on paper before driving around town conducting errands. Plan as many errands as possible for each outing.

"I can give you a six-word formula for success: Think things through then follow through."

Edward Rickenbacker

HABIT ~ 74

FOLLOW UP AND FOLLOW THROUGH

Some of the biggest gains in life can be achieved by simply following up with people and following through on ideas. Many people are good at starting projects, but success is reserved for those with the discipline to follow through.

"It is well to remember that
the entire universe, with
one trifling exception,
is composed of others."

John Andrew Holmes

HABIT ~ 75

LET GO OF SCHEDULING YOUR APPOINTMENTS

Allow your assistant or secretary to schedule your appointments for you. This can eliminate the confusion of two people trying to schedule appointments. The person scheduling your time can also help you to protect your time by only scheduling productive appointments.

"It's all to do with the training:
you can do a lot if you're
properly trained."

Elizabeth II

HABIT ~ 76

USE YOUR LUNCH TIME EFFECTIVELY

List all the things you could be doing with your lunch hour. Think in terms of your goals and recreational activities. Challenge yourself to do at least one of these items each week. Keep in mind that one hour per week equates to fifty-two hours a year. You'll be amazed at what you can achieve.

"To believe in the heroic creates heroes."

Benjamin Disraeli

HABIT ~ 77

ADOPT A SUCCESSFUL ROLE MODEL

What person do you want to emulate? For example, Martin Luther King Jr. modeled Henry David Thoreau, Mohandas Gandhi and Jesus Christ. Find a person who is a great time manager and do what they do. Whenever possible, ask for their advice on how to be more productive and efficient with your time and life. If you can't talk to these greats, read books and articles about those you admire with an eye toward emulation.

"How can you say luck and chance are the same thing? Chance is the first step you take, luck is what comes afterwards."

Amy Tan

HABIT ~ 78

CONFIRM YOUR APPOINTMENTS

One of the easiest ways to minimize confusion and wasting time is to confirm your appointments on the prior day. This ensures that you and the person with whom you are meeting have the correct time and place and are both still available. This habit also gives you a gentle reminder to be prepared so that you can make the most of appointments.

"Success, like happiness, cannot be pursued. It must ensue.
And it only does so as
the unintended side effect
of one's personal dedication to a
cause greater than oneself."

Viktor Frankl

HABIT ~ 79

WRITE AND MEMORIZE YOUR PERSONAL MISSION STATEMENT

A mission statement contains your vision and reflects your core values. It is your own personal constitution and helps you answer the age-old questions: "Why am I here?" and "What is my purpose in life?" Mission statements provide you with focus, direction and purpose. Yours should be the foundation on which to base your decisions, and ultimately, the direction of your life.

"Through imagination, we can visualize the uncreated worlds of potential that lie within us."

Stephen Covey

HABIT ~ 80

MAKE A LIST OF THE QUALITIES YOU WANT TO POSSESS

What qualities do you have to possess to achieve the life you want? Honesty? Commitment? Superior service? Persistence? Unconditional love? Leadership? Optimism? Teamwork? Confidence? Dynamism? Generosity? Excellence? Humility? Brainstorm as many qualities as you can, then prioritize the top three you're going to acquire.

"Wisdom and penetration are the fruit of experience, not the lessons of retirement and leisure. Great necessities call out great virtues."

Abigail Adams

HABIT ~ 81

WHEN IN DOUBT
ALWAYS DO THE RIGHT THING

Sometimes it seems that the easy way is the best path to follow, but don't be fooled by short-term gains. When in doubt always do what is right for everyone involved. This is a powerful mechanism that strengthens your personal integrity. Doing the right thing for the right reason influences your mind in a positive way. One of the extraordinary side effects of this habit is that you sleep better at night!

"Let all things
have their places."

Benjamin Franklin

HABIT ~ 82

FILE IMPORTANT ARTICLES AND EDUCATIONAL INFORMATION

Get your hands on the information you need when you need it. Clip magazine and newspaper articles that are of interest to you, then file them. This allows for easy reference on the topics that are of interest to you and your business. It also gets rid of clutter.

"Getting people to like you is simply the other side of liking other people."

Norman Vincent Peale

HABIT ~ 83

RELEASE YOURSELF FROM NEGATIVE JUDGMENT

When you judge a person it does not define them, it defines you as someone who needs to judge. Many people spend an enormous amount of time and energy judging other people. Spend your energy looking for the best in everyone by searching for the attributes you admire and respect. The most irritating traits in others are almost always the traits you refuse to see in yourself.

"The person who moved a mountain was the one who began carrying away small stones."

Chinese Proverb

HABIT ~ 84

USE YOUR TRANSITION TIME

Think of all the activities you can accomplish in five to ten minutes. Use this list during the day to make use of the small pockets of waiting time or transition time. Also list all of the things you can do while traveling in a car or on an airplane. Stop seeing time in the form of hours. By focusing in on smaller increments of time, you are able to focus in on smaller tasks—the ones that usually slip through the cracks or build up into larger tasks.

"The difference between getting somewhere and nowhere is the courage to make an early start."

Charles M. Schwab

HABIT ~ 85

WAKE AT THE SAME TIME EACH MORNING

Everything boils down to programming. When you set your alarm for the same time every day it helps to program your brain's sleeping cycle. Out of pure habit your brain will wake up at the same time. For some help in this area use an alarm system that turns on the lights, television, radio or pre-recorded sound to get you up and moving.

"Ability is what you're capable of doing. Motivation determines what you do. Attitude determines how well you do it."

Lou Holtz

HABIT ~ 86

KEEP YOUR THOUGHTS POSITIVE

You, and only you, can choose to keep your thoughts positive. This may require some effort at the beginning. However, taking control of your mind is empowering and critical to your life and time. Positive thoughts keep you in balance with the universe. Be aware of your inner dialog. Check in throughout the day to actually listen to the noise in your head. When what you hear is negative, make the effort to short-circuit the message and find one that is more positive. Do this often enough and, like all else, it becomes habit. Optimists aren't born, they're trained.

"Things which matter most
must never be at the mercy
of things which matter least."

Johann Goethe

HABIT ~ 87

GET YOUR PRIORITIES STRAIGHT

Learn to prioritize your most to least important actions. The act of writing down your priorities can bring life balance and peace. Once you have your list, plan time to focus on each priority, one at a time. A basic time management tool is to rate your items by categories in order of importance. Mark an "A" by vital, must be done items; a "B" for important tasks; and "C" for marginal, may be postponed tasks. Prioritizing forces you to really think about what is important to you and allows you to allocate time to those things you deem most necessary.

"I attribute my success
to this—
I never gave nor took
any excuse."

Florence Nightingale

HABIT ~ 88

USE A VOICE-RECORDER

Catch your own inspiration. Record your thoughts and flashes of insight on a voice-recorder. Authors, executives and great leaders often use this tool to ensure they capture moments of inspiration or key ideas to help them improve. Voice-recorders can also serve to dictate information to an assistant or secretary for all written correspondence. If you don't have the luxury of an assistant to type your recording, you can hire a transcriber for a nominal fee.

"Past successes are bridges
that lead us to our
next victory."

Jeffrey Lawrence Benjamin

HABIT ~ 89

REMEMBER YOUR PAST SUCCESSFUL EXPERIENCES

Everything we've heard, seen, touched, smelled or tasted is stored in our brain and nervous system. During the course of our life we record these experiences and constantly refer back to them to help us decipher and decide what is occurring in the here-and-now. The challenge most people face is that they are referencing the potentially negative experiences, which then leads to poor decisions and a limited life. The key is to script your powerful references pertaining to success and triumph so you can use them to empower you, both now and in the future.

"There are no roles here.
We're just trying to
accomplish something."

Thomas Edison

HABIT ~ 90

GET RID OF YOUR DESK

It is easy for the drawers in your desk to become hiding places for unfinished projects. Get rid of this temptation by getting rid of your desk. This simple idea will cause you to create better work habits such as touching a piece of paper only once, delegating projects that are best done by others, and keeping yourself free of distractions.

"When a man dies they who survive him ask what property he has left behind. The angel who bends over the dying man asks what good deeds he has sent before him."

The Koran

HABIT ~ 91

APPRECIATE ALL RELIGIONS

Religion turns into oppression when it stomps on another person's beliefs. For thousands of years ignorant people have fought and killed in the name of God. What purpose has this lack of acceptance served? Save time by accepting instead of wasting time fighting another person's beliefs. Base your acceptance of a belief system on whether its core message is founded on love and compassion. Better yet, base your acceptance on the fact that your own core message is founded on love and compassion.

"When you have cleared all of your clutter, you can be of greater service to those around you."

Michael B. Kitson

HABIT ~ 92

CLEAR THE CLUTTER

If you absolutely don't love something get rid of it. Sell, give, recycle or throw it away. Clutter clearing will open up incredible opportunities and possibilities by freeing up space in your life and mind. It allows the opportunity to give to charity, to rearrange your space and to examine your life. Clear your clutter daily. You will find you have much more time to get the important tasks completed when your space is clutter-free.

"When I was a boy of fourteen, my father was so ignorant I could hardly stand to have the old man around. But when I got to be twenty-one, I was astonished at how much he had learned in seven years."

Mark Twain

HABIT ~ 93

LEAVE CLEAR VOICEMAILS

The beauty of voicemail is that it enables you to leave clear messages with desired results for the recipient. Tell the person who you are, what you are looking to accomplish, and how they can help or how you can help them. Remember to always leave your phone number, along with your name, as the person listening to your message may be retrieving it from another location and may not have your number handy. For easy reference, leave your name and number first, so if the recipient has to review the message for this information he or she won't have to listen to your whole message again.

"Luck is not chance
It's Toil
Fortune's expensive smile
Is earned."

Emily Dickinson

HABIT ~ 94

REVIEW YOUR FINANCIAL STATUS

Many people obsess about money and their financial status. A regular monthly review of your financial plans can help relieve such anxiety. For example, set aside one hour the last Saturday or Sunday of each month for your personal financial review. Not only will this ease your mind, it will help you budget for the month ahead.

"The mind is everything.
What we think, we become."

Buddha

HABIT ~ 95

RATE YOUR PERFORMANCE

Have the courage to examine your daily, weekly, monthly and yearly progress. If you regularly write out your goals it will be easier to rate your performance. If you don't write your goals, start. You will probably find accomplishing anything long-term is easier when you take the time to see how your short-term steps are progressing.

"I think of true neurotics
as people who would rather
hold on to their illusion of
control than run the risk
of getting what they want."

Anne Wilson Schaef

HABIT ~ 96

PLAN YOUR WEEK, MONTH, QUARTER AND YEAR

To truly own your life you must take ownership of your time. Prioritize and block out estimated time slots for each area of your life. To get an overview of your time, start by using a twelve-month calendar to differentiate and plan in advance the days you choose to play, be highly productive and to clean up messes and organize. The annual calendar should be very generic with details growing as the time increments decrease.

"The first problem for all
of us, men and women,
is not to learn, but
to unlearn."

Gloria Steinem

HABIT ~ 97

KEEP NOTES ON THE CALLS YOU MAKE

The more you do the less reliable your memory becomes. The easiest way to avoid problems in the future is to keep notes regarding the conversations you have and the commitments you make. Use a pen and paper organizer or use software programs such as Outlook, Palm, Goldmine or ACT, which allow you to journal conversations in conjunction with updating your database and task list. Write it down and keep it organized. Not only will you save time, you will free up your brain for more important tasks.

"The simplest explanation
is always the most likely."

Agatha Christie

HABIT ~ 98

STICK TO YOUR SCHEDULE

Either you own your time or the rest of the world will grab it from you. When you put an appointment in your schedule you are planning in advance what you want to accomplish. In a sense you are taking ownership of that block of time. To retain ownership you must be diligent about sticking to your schedule. This clarifies to the world and your own consciousness that your time is valuable and you are the rightful owner of that asset.

"You don't get to choose how you're going to die, or when. You can only decide how you're going to live: Now."

Joan Baez

HABIT ~ 99

SCHEDULE IN REVERSE

The best way to set your priorities for today is by deciding the priorities for your entire life. Start with a vision of what you wish to accomplish during your time here. What do you want people to say about you at your funeral? This way as you work backwards from your yearly, monthly, weekly and then daily schedule, you are able to distinguish and prioritize the activities that take you closer to your goals.

"When we do the best we can,
we never know what miracle
is wrought in our life, or
in the life of another."

Helen Keller

HABIT ~ 100

SET AND MEET DEADLINES

Completion dates can be very motivating. If you delegate a project make sure you deliver it with a deadline. Likewise, if someone asks you to do something, it's a good idea to ask the deadline. Deadlines seem to provide you with focused concentration and the momentum to get a job done. Do your best to meet all you set.

"Courage is more
exhilarating than fear,
and in the long run
it is easier."

Eleanor Roosevelt

HABIT ~ 101

ASSESS YOUR STRENGTHS AND WEAKNESSES

Know thyself is a mantra that has been echoed for thousands of years. The trouble is that most people are afraid to look within, fearing what they might find. If that describes you, get over it! Grab a piece of paper and draw a line down the middle. On one side list your strengths, the other your weaknesses. Be honest with yourself. Examine your list when you are finished, then resolve to accentuate your strengths and minimize your weaknesses.

Write your own habits for maximizing time…

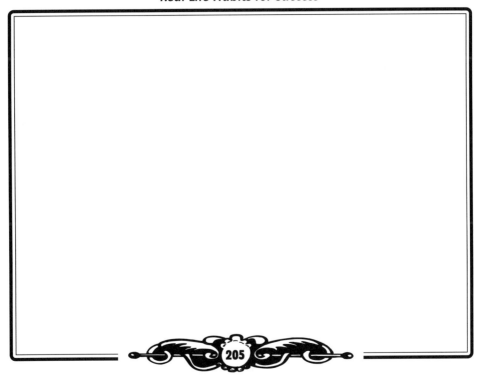

Real Life Habits for Success

Maximize Your Time

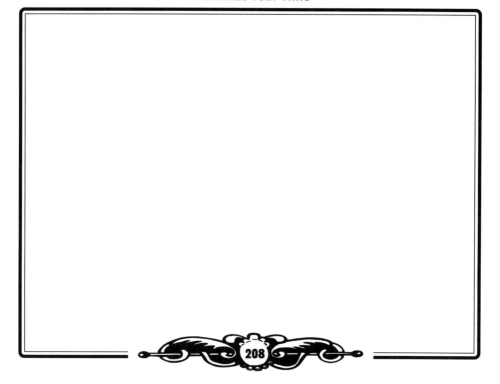

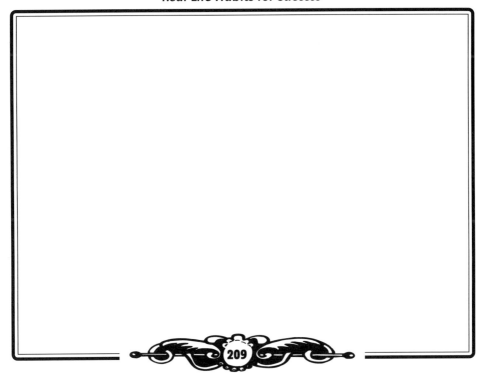

J. T. and Lindé Ravizé have used their superlative photography and poetry to encourage legislators and the public towards exceptional stewardship of the natural environment. Their award winning work is being used extensively to support efforts to preserve Lake Tahoe, Big Sur, Wine Country, and other imperiled natural places.

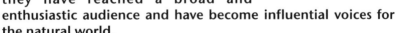

Using their "Hearts of Light" book series, and museum shows around the country, they have reached a broad and enthusiastic audience and have become influential voices for the natural world.

Visit their website: www.aframeofmind.com
E-mail: jtr@aframeofmind.com
Or call their gallery "A Frame of Mind Gallery" 775-588-8081

Jeffrey Benjamin

For more than 15 years author and speaker Jeffrey Benjamin has dedicated his life to passionately sharing career and personal achievement strategies with both small and large companies. He published his first book at the age of 23 and is the co-author of the acclaimed book series *Real Life Habits for Success*. He is also the host of his own television and radio show featuring leaders with real life success stories. Jeffrey is the founder of BREAKTHROUGH TRAINING, and a performance coach energizing thousands of people every month.

www.breakthroughtraining.com
toll free: 800.547.9868

Training & Coaching
Keynotes & Retreats

Mike Kitson

Mike is the founder and president of On-Call Graphics, Inc., a full-service creative studio in Reno, Nevada. OCG's mission is to work as a team, attract clients we enjoy, deliver uncompromising quality in a relaxing and creative environment. Mike holds his B.A. in Journalism from the University of Nevada. He has published over 20 books.

He is also the founder of the Forward Thinking Group, a group of consultants and coaches offering "Therapy for Business."

ON-CALL GRAPHICS | INC.
DESIGNING A BETTER IMAGE

www.oncallgraphics.com
toll free: 800.825.0448

John Oliver

John Oliver's work has taken him around the world and his diverse educational background includes degrees in Criminal Justice, English Literature and Kinesiology. John shares this knowledge and his experiences in life and business with individuals and fortune 500 companies.

John is a successful entrepreneur and is the keynote speaker, writer, and LifeCoach that helps you experience the joy of everyday life.

JohnOliver.com

Thomas J. Powell

Tom Powell is passionate about putting people into homes and helping them realize the American dream of homeownership. He is the President of *Into*homes Mortgage Services LLC, one of the leading mortgage lenders in Nevada. He speaks regularly to business, educational and community groups on success, motivation and leadership. He attributes his own success to constant investment in personal and professional development, both for himself and his employees. He shares a home with his wife and four children.

*into*homes toll free: 877-*into*homes *into*homes.*com*

Order Form

Please send me Maximizing Your Time for $8.95 per book plus shipping:

Quantity: $8.95 per book .... _____

Shipping: $2.00 per book .... _____

Total cost of book(s) and shipping cost: .... _____

For large quantity orders (10) books or more, please call 800.825.0448 for special discount pricing.

Full Name: _____

Mailing Address: _____

City: _____ State: _____ Zip: _____

MC/VISA/AMEX# _____ Exp._____

Check / Money Order for $_____ Payable to: World Vision Publishing, LLC

Daytime telephone number: (   ) _____

Signature: _____

Mail to: World View Publishing, P.O. Box 7332, Reno, Nevada, 89510.
Or call: 800.825.0448 to place your order today!

216